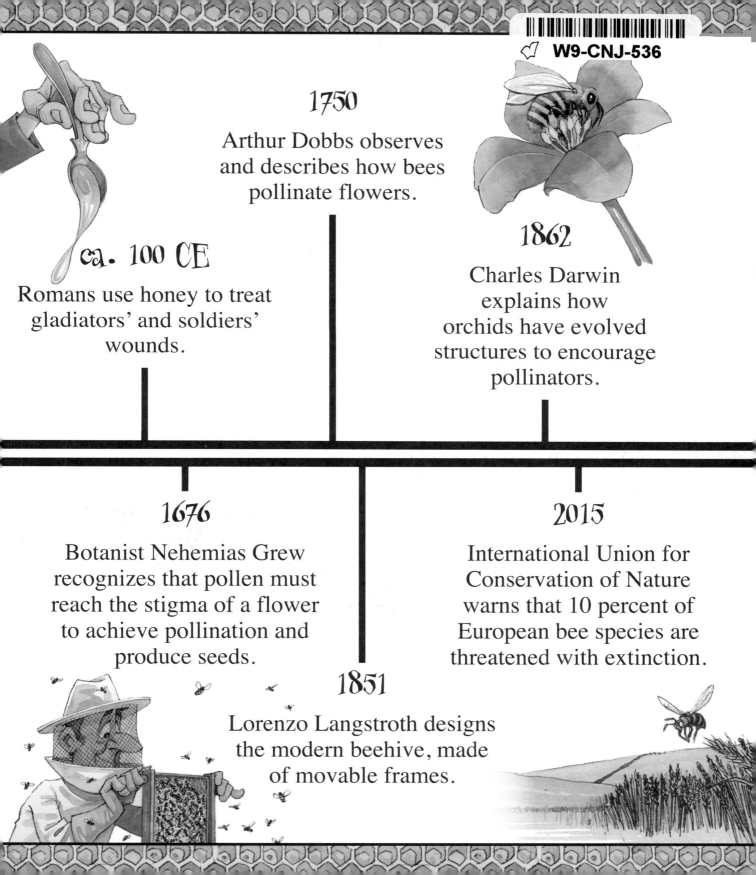

ca. 100 CE

Romans use honey to treat gladiators' and soldiers' wounds.

1676

Botanist Nehemias Grew recognizes that pollen must reach the stigma of a flower to achieve pollination and produce seeds.

1750

Arthur Dobbs observes and describes how bees pollinate flowers.

1851

Lorenzo Langstroth designs the modern beehive, made of movable frames.

1862

Charles Darwin explains how orchids have evolved structures to encourage pollinators.

2015

International Union for Conservation of Nature warns that 10 percent of European bee species are threatened with extinction.

Anatomy of a Honeybee

The honeybee is perfectly adapted to its way of life. It has special organs that allow it to fly, see, smell, gather and store nectar, collect pollen, and protect the hive. Like all insects, its body is made up of three main parts: the head, thorax, and abdomen. The head contains its brain, mouthparts, and sense organs; the thorax supports its wings and legs; and the abdomen contains important organs like its heart, honey stomach, intestines, and stinger.

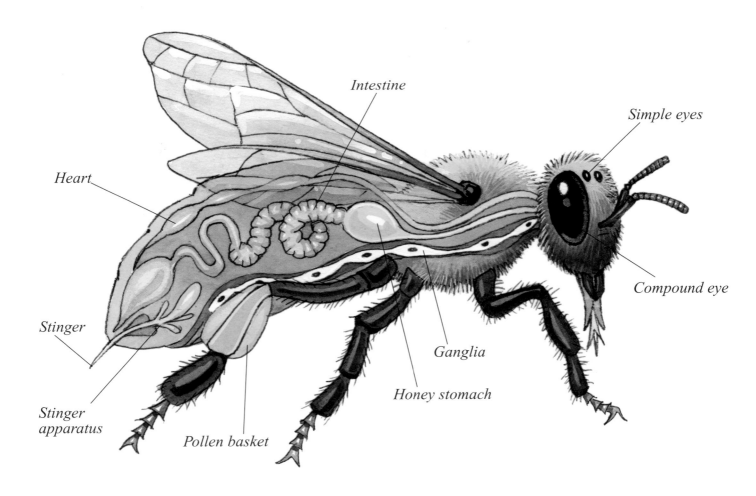

Intestine

Simple eyes

Heart

Compound eye

Stinger

Ganglia

Honey stomach

Stinger apparatus

Pollen basket

Author:

Alex Woolf studied history at Essex University, England. He is the author of over 60 books for children, many of them on historical topics. They include *You Wouldn't Want to Live Without Books!,* *You Wouldn't Want to Live Without Poop!,* and *You Wouldn't Want to Live Without Vegetables!*

Artist:

David Antram was born in Brighton, England, in 1958. He studied at Eastbourne College of Art and then worked in advertising for 15 years before becoming a full-time artist. He has illustrated many children's nonfiction books.

Series creator:

David Salariya was born in Dundee, Scotland. He has illustrated a wide range of books and has created and designed many new series for publishers in the UK and overseas. David established The Salariya Book Company in 1989. He lives in Brighton, England, with his wife, illustrator Shirley Willis, and their son, Jonathan.

Editor: **Jacqueline Ford**

Editorial Assistant: **Mark Williams**

PAPER FROM
SUSTAINABLE
FORESTS

Published in Great Britain in 2017 by
The Salariya Book Company Ltd
25 Marlborough Place, Brighton BN1 1UB

ISBN-13: 978-0-531-22458-8 (lib. bdg.) 978-0-531-22487-8 (pbk.)

All rights reserved.
Published in 2017 in the United States
by Franklin Watts
An imprint of Scholastic Inc.

A CIP catalog record for this book is available
from the Library of Congress.

Printed and bound in China.
Printed on paper from sustainable sources.

1 2 3 4 5 6 7 8 9 10 R 26 25 24 23 22 21 20 19 18 17

You Wouldn't Want to Live Without™

Bees!

Written by
Alex Woolf

Illustrated by
David Antram

Series created by
David Salariya

Franklin Watts®
An Imprint of Scholastic Inc.

Contents

Introduction

What would happen if there were no bees in this world? It would be a disaster! Without bees, we would, of course, have no honey. But we'd also lose a lot of other foods produced by plants that bees pollinate. Around half the fruit and vegetables in our supermarkets would disappear! Not only that, we would also lose the animals that eat these plants, and the animals that eat those animals! As far as important species are concerned, bees are at the top of the list. You really wouldn't want to live without them.

What Is a Bee?

Bees are flying insects. They are closely related to wasps and ants. In fact, bees evolved from wasps. Bees feed on nectar and pollen, which they obtain from flowering plants. They get their energy from nectar. Most of the pollen is given as food to their larvae. Many species of bee live together in colonies. These social bees are highly organized, hardworking, and intelligent. Some kinds of social bees, like honeybees, keep busy all summer collecting enough food for the winter.

I can't believe I'm related to wasps!

BEEKEEPING. Humans have been keeping bees for thousands of years. They keep them in hives in order to collect their honey and to pollinate their crops.

Here we go again!

The thief!

Top Tip

How to tell a bee from a wasp: Bees have more bristles on their bodies. Bees have combs on their forelimbs for cleaning their antennae. Most bees collect pollen, while most wasps don't.

Try some.

After you.

You can now see the future.

Is the future good for bees?

Gotcha!

HONEY was used as a sweetener long before sugar was common. If it's kept sealed, honey doesn't spoil. Jars of honey found in Egyptian tombs are still edible thousands of years later.

MYTHOLOGY. In ancient Greek mythology, the god Apollo received the gift of prophecy from three bee goddesses. Bees also appear in Egyptian, African, and Asian myths.

PREDATORS. Bees are preyed on by birds such as the bee-eater; insects including dragonflies and beewolves; and mammals such as honey badgers, skunks, weasels, foxes, bears, and shrews.

What Are the Parts of a Bee?

Forewing

Let's take a closer look at the bee, so we can see how it uses the different parts of its body. A major part of a bee's life involves collecting nectar and pollen from flowering plants, and its body is well adapted for this task. The bee's body is protected by an exoskeleton (a hard covering). It's also covered with lots of fuzzy hair for collecting pollen and regulating body temperature.

Hindwing

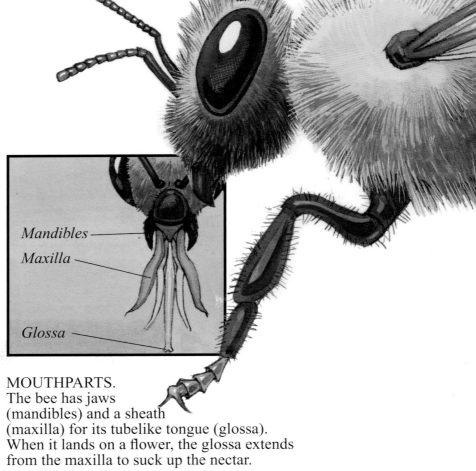

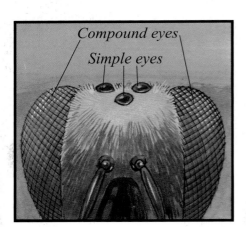

Compound eyes
Simple eyes

Mandibles
Maxilla
Glossa

BEE EYES. Bees have five eyes: three simple eyes for detecting light, and two large compound eyes, made up of thousands of eye cells, used for detecting movement and patterns.

MOUTHPARTS. The bee has jaws (mandibles) and a sheath (maxilla) for its tubelike tongue (glossa). When it lands on a flower, the glossa extends from the maxilla to suck up the nectar.

8

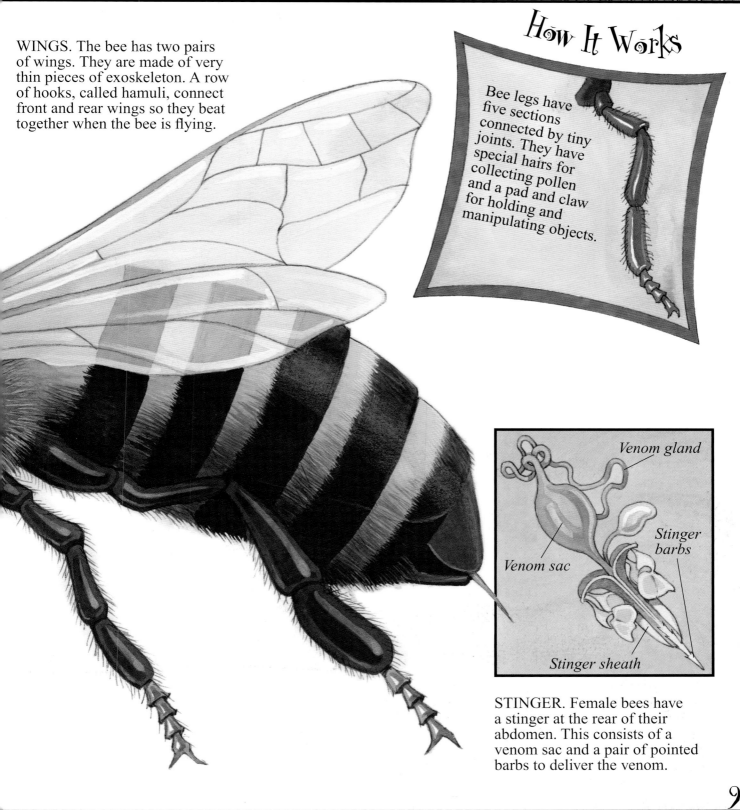

WINGS. The bee has two pairs of wings. They are made of very thin pieces of exoskeleton. A row of hooks, called hamuli, connect front and rear wings so they beat together when the bee is flying.

How It Works

Bee legs have five sections connected by tiny joints. They have special hairs for collecting pollen and a pad and claw for holding and manipulating objects.

Venom gland

Venom sac

Stinger barbs

Stinger sheath

STINGER. Female bees have a stinger at the rear of their abdomen. This consists of a venom sac and a pair of pointed barbs to deliver the venom.

9

Are There Different Types of Bees?

There are more than 20,000 species of bee—and those are just the ones we know about! You can tell bee species apart by their physical characteristics, like wing shape or tongue length. Some species, including honeybees, bumblebees, and stingless bees, are social creatures living in colonies. Others, like the carpenter bee, live solitary lives. Most people are familiar with social bees because they are more visible. However, only 15 percent of all bees are social.

BIG AND SMALL. Bees range in size from the mighty Megachile pluto, which can reach 1.6 inches (4 centimeters) in length, to a tiny species of stingless bee, less than 0.08 inches (2 millimeters) long.

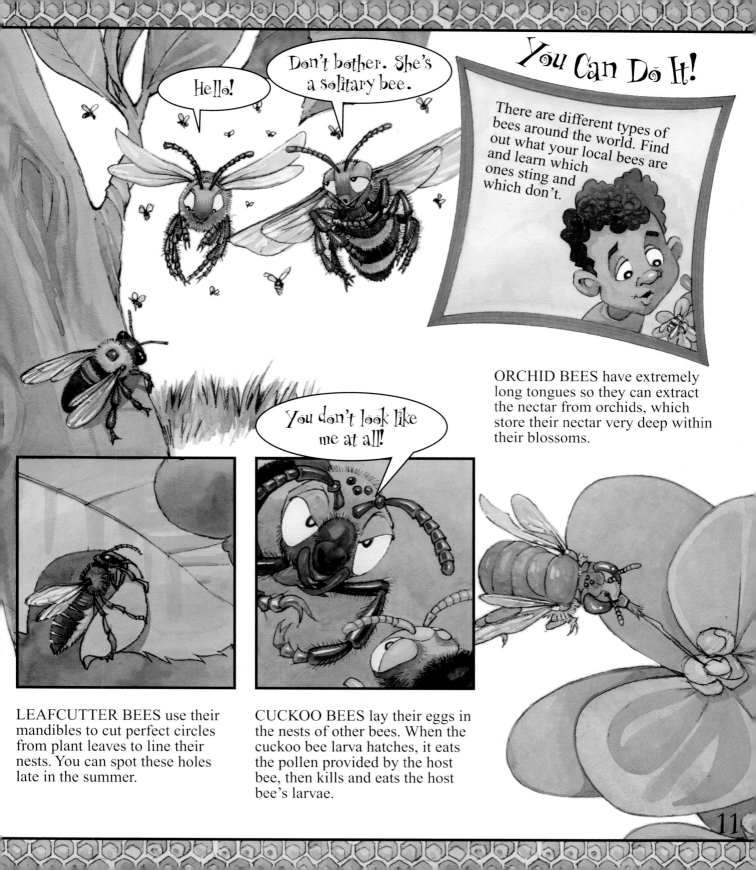

Hello!

Don't bother. She's a solitary bee.

You Can Do It!

There are different types of bees around the world. Find out what your local bees are and learn which ones sting and which don't.

ORCHID BEES have extremely long tongues so they can extract the nectar from orchids, which store their nectar very deep within their blossoms.

You don't look like me at all!

LEAFCUTTER BEES use their mandibles to cut perfect circles from plant leaves to line their nests. You can spot these holes late in the summer.

CUCKOO BEES lay their eggs in the nests of other bees. When the cuckoo bee larva hatches, it eats the pollen provided by the host bee, then kills and eats the host bee's larvae.

11

Why Do Flowers Need Bees?

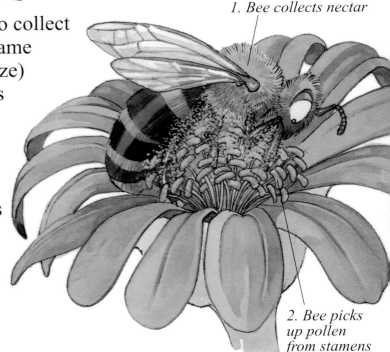

1. Bee collects nectar

2. Bee picks up pollen from stamens

Bees visit flowering plants to collect nectar and pollen. At the same time, they pollinate (fertilize) the plants. While the bee is collecting the nectar and pollen, some pollen from the stamen (male part of the flower) sticks to the hairs of her body. When she visits the next flower, some of this pollen is rubbed off onto the stigma (top of the female part of the flower). This fertilizes the plant and causes it to produce seeds and fruit.

COLOR. Bees are attracted to a flower by its color, shape, and scent. Since bees can't see red, they are most attracted to yellow, blue, purple, and white flowers.

NECTAR GUIDES. Some flowers have nectar guides—patterns to guide bees to the nectar. The patterns are visible only in ultraviolet, a form of light not visible to humans.

TONGUE. The bee's tongue is covered with bristles that extend outward to catch the nectar. The bee sucks its tongue back in with the nectar on it. It does this in less than half a second.

3. Pollen-covered bee visits another flower

4. Pollen gets rubbed off on stigma

You Can Do It!

Look closely at different flowers with a magnifying glass. Can you find the pollen? Some flowers, such as lilies, have long anthers and it's easy to brush the pollen off with your fingers. It's harder with asters.

Bravo! Now where's the nectar?

POLLEN BASKETS. Some bees use their forelegs to brush pollen from their body to their back legs, then they compress it in "pollen baskets" to carry back to the hive.

Pollen basket

NAVIGATION. The bee's internal clock tells it how far it's flown and how far the Sun has moved during its journey, so that it can always find its way back home to the hive.

BEE DANCE. Honeybees return to the hive and do a dance to show other bees where to find nectar. Their movements tell these other bees the direction to fly in relation to the Sun, and the distance.

What Is Life Like in the Hive?

Honeybee hives are busy places, with different bees performing particular tasks. Hives contain around 20,000 to 30,000 bees. These are made up of female workers, male drones, and a queen. The workers do all the work in the hive. The drones, however, have just one function and that is to mate with the queen. They do no work in the hive and are usually there only during late spring and summer.

It's a hard life being a drone.

I can see *that!*

JOBS IN THE HIVE. The queen bee lays all the eggs. She can lay 1,500 a day—more than her body weight—and up to a million during her lifetime. Young workers build and repair the beeswax comb of hexagonal cells for storing honey, pollen, and larvae. They clean the nest, feed the larvae, care for the queen, remove waste, handle incoming nectar, and guard the entrance.

JOBS OUTSIDE THE HIVE. Older worker bees go out and collect nectar, pollen, and water.

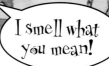

How It Works

For a hive to function, the bees have to communicate. They do this through dances and by producing a chemical called a pheromone.

I smell what you mean!

Do you love me, Mom?

You're one in a million!

Eat up, Your Majesty!

Hope I'm a worker.

Hope I'm a drone.

BEE BABIES. Larvae are fed a special substance called royal jelly for three days, then they are given a mixture of nectar and pollen called bee bread.

QUEEN CELL. A larger cell is made to hold a future queen bee. The larva of the future queen is given a different diet, with more royal jelly.

THE CHANGE. When the larva is big enough, workers cap its cell with wax, and the larva pupates. When it's ready to emerge, the pupa chews through the wax lid and joins the community.

15

Why Do Bees Swarm?

A whirling mass of swarming bees can be a scary sight, yet it's a natural part of the life cycle of honeybees. When a colony gets too big, the queen's pheromone signals can no longer reach all the workers. For those who don't receive the signals, it's as if the queen doesn't exist—so they start raising new queen larvae. Before the new queens hatch, the old queen departs the nest with her loyal followers gathered tightly around her in a swarm.

WEAK FLYER. The queen is not a strong flyer, so the swarm will have to rest at some point, on a tree branch or fence. Scouts are then sent out to search for a suitable place for a nest.

NEW NEST. Scouts do a waggle dance to tell the others about a nest site. The more a scout likes a site, the more excited her dance. Eventually, a favorite site is decided on, and the swarm flies there.

Good shelter? Near flowers? Sounds great!

16

It's all right, they're just moving to a new home.

I'm queen!

No, I am!

FIGHT TO THE DEATH. Back at the old hive, the newly hatched queens do battle until one remains. She becomes the new queen.

BEE BEARDS. Trained beekeepers sometimes compete to get the best bee beard. They put a queen bee in a cage around their necks and wait for the worker bees to cluster above her.

17

How Do Bees Make Honey?

Bees are best known for making honey. They use it as food for the hive during the winter months. The first stage of honey-making is collecting the nectar. The nectar they choose will affect the color and flavor of the honey. Orange blossom honey, for example, tastes faintly of oranges. The bees store the nectar in their honey stomach, which is next to their regular stomach. Nectar is about 70 percent water. To turn it into honey, the bees must reduce the water content to about 20 percent.

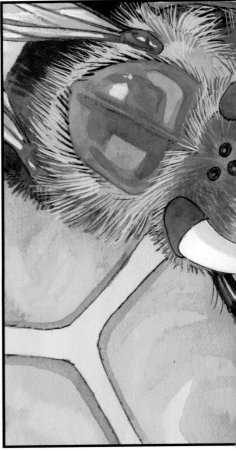

1. REGURGITATING. The bee takes the nectar back to the nest and regurgitates it into another bee's mouth. The bees in the hive turn the nectar into honey by chewing, swallowing, and regurgitating it over and over.

So honey is basically bee vomit?

Well, not exactly...

There you go.

Thank you!

You Can Do It!

Do your part to help bees. Plant flowers that attract bees, either in a corner of your garden or in a window box. They like blue and yellow flowers best!

2. FANNING. The honey is still very wet, so the workers fan their wings over the filled cells of the honeycomb to evaporate more water from it.

3. CAPPING. When the honey is ready, the bees seal the cell with a wax lid to keep it clean. The finished honey is thick, sticky, and very sweet.

HARD WORK. It takes eight bees all their lives to make just one teaspoonful of honey! Think about that the next time you eat some honey....

19

What Do Beekeepers Do?

People have collected honey from wild hives for at least ten thousand years. Gradually, people figured out how to keep bees in artificial hives. They learned more about the behavior of bees and how to exploit this to increase honey yields. For example, skilled beekeepers need to ensure that their hives have lots of foraging bees just when the local flowers are producing the most nectar. They need to manage the swarming instinct, so they don't lose half their bees at the wrong moment. It takes many years of experience to be a successful beekeeper.

LANGSTROTH HIVE. Modern hives are made with removable frames to hold honey and for bees to raise their brood. The most common is the Langstroth hive, developed in the 1850s by Lorenzo Langstroth, a minister who became a beekeeper.

Of course my bees aren't going to swarm.

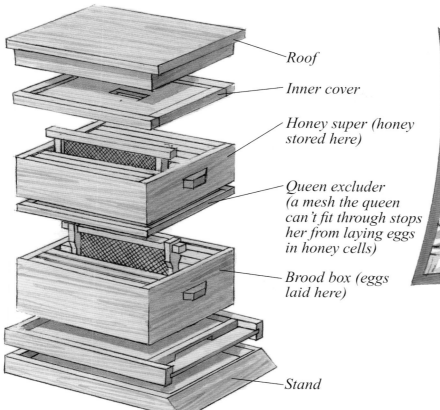

Roof

Inner cover

Honey super (honey stored here)

Queen excluder (a mesh the queen can't fit through stops her from laying eggs in honey cells)

Brood box (eggs laid here)

Stand

Most beekeepers use a hood and gloves to protect their face and hands from stings while working on their hives.

ANCIENT EGYPTIANS kept bees 4,000 years ago. Cylindrical hives made of clay were stacked in rows up to 8 feet (2.4 meters) high.

SMOKE. Since ancient times, beekeepers have used smoke to calm the bees while they take the honey. Smoke causes bees to gorge on honey, making them fat and slow.

WILD HONEY. Harvesting honey from wild bee nests is still practiced today by indigenous peoples in many parts of the world.

How Else Do Bees Help Us?

The most important job that bees do is pollinating flowers. Honey is an added bonus! But bees can be helpful in other ways as well. For example, "beehive fences" are used in Africa to keep elephants from trampling farmland. Fields are surrounded by beehives hung from wires. If an elephant touches the wire, the hives shake and the bees come out, which drives the elephants away. The beehive fence is a bit like an electric fence, but it's cheaper, it doesn't hurt the elephants, and honey and pollinators come with it.

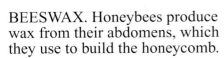

BEESWAX. Honeybees produce wax from their abdomens, which they use to build the honeycomb. We can melt this wax and use it to make candles, cosmetics, shoe polish, and even surfboard wax.

Honey is a good remedy for sore throats and mouth ulcers. It draws water out of inflamed tissue, reducing swelling and discomfort.

This might sting a bit!

I love honey!

How sweet!

HONEY TREATMENT. Honey has germ-killing properties, and has been used to treat wounds for thousands of years.

FUNGICIDE. Researchers have experimented with using bees to deliver fungicide to plants. The bees walk through a tray of fungicide powder as they leave the hive and carry it to flowers.

VENOM MEDICINE. Bee venom sounds nasty, but chemicals extracted from it have been used to treat conditions like nerve pain and multiple sclerosis.

What Dangers Do Bees Face?

Bees have always faced dangers from predators, disease, and parasites. But now they face threats from humans as well—from pesticides, loss of habitat, and pollution. In 2006, beekeepers noticed a new and disturbing trend. In honeybee colonies in North America and Europe, worker bees were disappearing, leaving behind the queen and a few nurse bees. Without nectar-gatherers, the colonies soon died. This became known as Colony Collapse Disorder (CCD). Scientists suspect CCD is caused by a combination of parasites, pesticides, and poor diet.

I don't feel too good....

Where have all the flowers gone?

PARASITES. Varroa mites attach to a honeybee's body and suck its blood, killing many bees and spreading disease. The varroa can jump from one colony to another, wiping out vast numbers of bees.

POOR DIET. Bees need a varied diet of different pollens. The loss of hedges and meadows and the planting of a single crop over large areas makes it harder for bee colonies to survive.

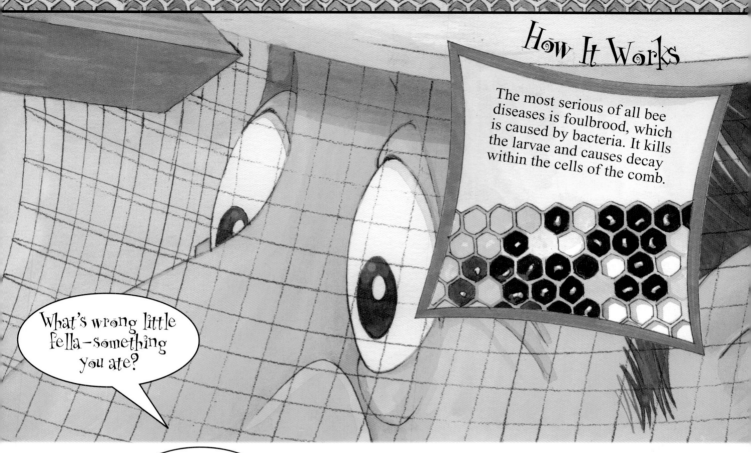

How It Works

The most serious of all bee diseases is foulbrood, which is caused by bacteria. It kills the larvae and causes decay within the cells of the comb.

What's wrong little fella—something you ate?

I can't smell a thing.

POLLUTION. Tests have shown that chemicals from vehicle exhaust can alter the scent of flowers, making it harder for bees to locate food sources.

Cough! Cough!

PESTICIDES. Farmers spray chemicals on their crops to protect them from insect pests and diseases. Pesticides called neonicotinoids may be very harmful to bees.

Do Bees Kill?

The vast majority of bees are peaceful creatures, who will sting only if threatened. However, there is one species—the Africanized honeybee, also known as the "killer bee"—that is more dangerous. This species originated in 1956 in Brazil, where African and European bees were crossbred. Killer bees are very sensitive to the presence of humans and it doesn't take much to trigger their alarm pheromones. They attack in swarms of tens of thousands of bees.

To bee, or not to bee?

BEE STINGS. Honeybees die after stinging because their stingers have barbs on them. The barbs get stuck on the person stung, and when the bees try to fly off after stinging, part of their abdomen is ripped away. Other bee species have smooth stingers and can sting many times.

Capture the queen! It's the only way to stop them!

We like to offer a warm welcome!

BEE BALL. Hornets often attack beehives for their larvae. The bees defend themselves by surrounding the hornet in a tight "bee ball" of up to 500 bees, raising the temperature inside and slowly cooking the hornet.

You Can Do It!

If you are stung by a bee, don't try to pull the stinger out with your fingers, because this may release more venom. Scrape or flick it off with your fingernail or any flat edge.

How am I supposed to do that?

ALLERGIES. Some people are allergic to bee stings. Their throat can swell up, making it hard to breathe, and they can get skin rashes. People who are allergic to bees are advised to carry a shot of medicine that can stop an allergic reaction.

Would You Really Want to Live Without Bees?

A world without bees would be pretty grim. So many of the fruits and vegetables we enjoy wouldn't exist without the pollinating efforts of bees. Neither would honey or beeswax. And we're only starting to discover all sorts of other uses for bees, from delivering fungicide to keeping elephants away from crops. As much as we do know about bees that makes us treasure them, there may be much more that we can still learn from these amazingly busy, intelligent, and selfless insects and the complex world of the beehive.

A hive of bees will fly 25,000 miles (40,000 km) and visit a million flowers to produce 2 pounds (1 kilogram) of honey.

Busy, aren't they!

FOOD CHAIN. It's not only humans that benefit from bees. Several species of birds, spiders, and insects depend on bees as part of their diet. Also, animals like bears and honey badgers love eating honey.

Honey tastes great, but there's usually a sting in the tail!

You Can Do It!

Ask if you can put a bee nest in your garden. It will give solitary bees somewhere to spend the winter. You can buy one or make your own from bamboo or piping.

You never visit me anymore.

Sorry, my tongue's too short.

BEE-FRIENDLY GARDENS. People can help bees by planting bee-friendly flowers, vegetables, and herbs, such as lilac, lavender, wisteria, squash, pumpkins, sunflowers, and honeysuckle.

IN TOWNS AND CITIES people are trying their hand at beekeeping. "City bees" are often healthier than "rural bees" because there are fewer pesticides in city gardens.

GLOBAL WARMING has reduced flower populations in the Rocky Mountains. Over many generations, bees have adapted by developing shorter tongues, so they can suck nectar from more flowers.

Glossary

Abdomen The hindmost section of an insect's body, containing most of its organs.

Allergic Relating to an allergy—a damaging reaction by the body to a substance, such as bee venom.

Antenna (plural: **antennae**) Either of a pair of long, thin appendages on the heads of insects, used for sensing.

Bacteria Single-celled microorganisms, some of which can cause disease.

Beeswax The wax secreted by bees to make honeycomb.

Colony A community of animals, such as bees, living close together and forming an organized unit.

Drone In a colony of social bees, a male bee that does no work but can fertilize a queen.

Foraging Searching widely for food in the wild.

Fungicide A chemical that destroys fungus—a type of organism that can cause disease.

Global warming A gradual increase in the overall temperature of Earth's atmosphere, generally accepted as caused by increased levels of carbon dioxide.

Hexagonal Describing a hexagon, a shape that has six straight sides of equal length.

Honeycomb A structure of hexagonal cells of wax, made by bees to store honey and eggs.

Indigenous Living or growing naturally in a particular place.

Larva (plural: **larvae**) The young form of an insect, often wingless and wormlike, and very different from its parents at birth. The larval stage is the stage between egg and pupa.

Mandibles Either half of the crushing organ in the mouth parts of an insect.

Nectar A sugary fluid secreted within flowers to encourage pollination by insects, and collected by bees in order to make honey.

Parasite An organism that lives in or on another organism (its host) and benefits by obtaining nutrients at the host's expense.

Pesticide A substance used to destroy insects and other organisms harmful to cultivated plants.

Pheromone A chemical released by an animal affecting the behavior of others of its species.

Pollen A fine powdery substance, typically yellow, discharged from the male part of a flower (stamen). It contains cells that can fertilize the stigma, which is the top part of the female part of a flower (pistil).

Pollination The transferral of pollen from flower to flower by wind, insects, or other animals to allow fertilization.

Pupa The stage of an insect between larva and becoming an adult, usually while enclosed in a case or a cocoon.

Pupate (Of a larva) Become a pupa.

Regurgitate Bring (swallowed food) up again to the mouth.

Thorax The middle section of an insect's body, between the head and the abdomen, that bears the legs and wings.

Ultraviolet A form of radiation that has a wavelength shorter than that of visible light, so cannot be seen by humans.

Index

Top Honeybee Talents

1. Their wings beat 200 times a second, creating that familiar buzzing sound. They fly at an average of 15 miles (24 km) an hour.

2. They can recognize human faces. They take individual parts, like eyebrows, lips, and ears, and pull them all together to make out the whole face.

3. They have 170 odor receptors, compared to just 62 in fruit flies. This enables them to smell the difference between hundreds of different types of flowers.

4. They can perceive the difference between images in one 300th of a second, compared to just a 50th of a second for humans. So if a honeybee watched television, it would see each individual frame.

5. The queen has control over whether she lays male or female eggs.

6. Worker bees' jobs change as they age: From 1 to 2 days old, they clean the hive; from 3 to 11 days, they feed larvae; from 12 to 21 days, they build combs, eject sick or dead bees from the hive, and act as guards; from 22 days until their death, they go out and forage.

7. They can figure out the shortest route between different nectar sources to minimize flying time. This highly complex mathematical task is calculated by their tiny brains, which are the size of a sesame seed.

The Bee Dance

When a bee locates a new food source, it returns to the hive and hands out samples of the flower's nectar to other members of the hive. Then it performs a dance that indicates the distance, direction, quality, and quantity of the food supply. There are two kinds of dance: the round dance and the waggle dance.

The Round Dance

With the "round dance," the bee turns in circles to the left and to the right. This is performed if the food source is less than 105 feet (32 m) away. The better the food source, the longer and more excited the dance. The round dance doesn't tell the bees what direction to fly in, but the bees will recognize the smell from their nectar samples, so they will know how to find the flowers.

The Waggle Dance

With the "waggle dance," the bee does two loops with a straight run in the middle. This is performed if the food source is more than 105 feet (32 m) away. The rate of looping indicates the distance to the food source. The faster the rate, the closer the food supply. The bee also buzzes as it loops, and this is another indicator of distance: The longer it buzzes, the farther away the food is.

The direction of the straight run demonstrates the direction the bees should fly in, relative to the Sun. If the food is in the same direction as the Sun, the bee dances straight up. If it lies in the opposite direction of the Sun, the bee dances straight down. If it's to the right, the bee dances at the appropriate angle to the right, and so on